A YEAR OF HAIKU

By

Daphne Ashling Purpus

DEDICATION

This collection is dedicated to my dearest fur friends, past and present: Marmalade, Tabitha, Abbey, Shosty, Sasha, Thackeray, Laoise, Chauncey, Poosa, Oliver, and Calliope. Thank you for keeping me grounded and present, teaching me what is really important.

ACKNOWLEDGEMENTS

I have been helped and inspired by many people. First I want to thank Michael Dylan Welch for founding National Haiku Writing Month and setting up the Facebook page NaHaiWriMo, which began in 2010 with the idea of writing a haiku a day in the month of February, the shortest genre of poetry for the shortest month of the year. I wrote my first haiku on February 1, 2010 as NaHaiWriMo began, and I have written at least one haiku each and every day since then. I have been inspired and supported on my journey by the many wonderful haiku poets who participate in NaHaiWriMo, which has continued without pause since that first day.

I would also like to thank my internet friends Peter Scott and Lydia Schoch for their encouragement. I would like to thank Satayana Fiona Robyn and Kaspalita Thompson for their online classes at Writing Our Way Home and for publishing several of my haiku in the two books containing small stones which they have edited: Pay Attention: A River of Small Stones (Lulu.com, 2011) and A Blackbird Sings: A Book of Short Poems (Woodsmoke Press, 2012). Two of the poems in this book were previously published in A Blackbird Sings: "catching snowflakes" (pg. 71) and "shoveling snow" (pg. 38).

Finally, most of all, I would like to thank my friends and colleagues on Vashon who have encouraged me with their words and their belief in me and my artistic talents. There are many in this group, *but I would especially like to mention Cynthia Zheutlin, Nan Hammett, Kathy Wheaton, Leigh Moorhouse, Anja Moritz, and all my students from Student Link, Vashon High School, and the Senior Center Bridge Class. Your support of my endeavors is beyond price.*

JANUARY

the mermaid and I
washing hair
New Year's Day

through the firs
sunlight dapples
the rainbow flag

A Year of Haiku

pouring rain
on the skylights
a cat purrs

snuggling with
cats and dogs
the wind howls

winter break ends
as students return
a mug of hot tea

a vet visit
furry friends
clamor for treats

a cold crisp day
outside the window
a hummingbird

tutoring math
the students' eyes glaze
daydreaming

teleporting
past brake lights
my thoughts

twelve muddy
cocker paws
winter rains

A Year of Haiku

walking
to the mailbox
surrounded by pines

pinks and oranges
watching the sunrise
through the firs

a full moon
behind the firs
the dog barks

the ailing cat
starts eating
a sunny winter day

soaking
in the hot tub
firs dancing

catching snowflakes
on my tongue
hot tub soak

the ground slides
a teetering
friendship

snow draping
over bare branches
evergreens droop

birds chirping
four different songs
hot tub music

the cyclamen peeks
out of a thick
snow blanket

holiday lights
shining through
snow cover

ice storms
and heavy snows
freshly baked brownies

snow covered bushes
faerie homes with
twinkling lights

shoveling snow
for the last time
again

snow melting
from tree branches
a squirrel jumps

rain soaked snow
sliding off
the metal roof

a new haircut
for a new year
dragons soar overhead

geese honk above the hot tub

pouring rain
soaking in
the hot tub

colored lights
twinkling
crescent moon

dragons
breathing fire
my son runs 100 miles

FEBRUARY

listening to rags
quilting up a
storm

two perfect
geometry exams
a teacher's apple

waves of light
a cat sails through
dental surgery

three dogs
racing downhill chasing
nothing

hatching
quilt designs
hot tub soak

centered
in the kitchen window
a full moon

the mother
I never knew
a bee in the hellebore

a student's hat
filled with buttons
geometry lesson

winter
nearly iceless
a cyclamen blooms

evening walk
to the hot tub
a snail

piecing
quilt squares
fresh olive bread

cats watching
the front loader spin
pouring rain

mountains
reflecting the sunrise
a dog barks

a slug
crosses a hellebore
valentine hug

pools of green
shining in a sea
of black fur

an endless
queue of raindrops
winter break begins

the wind
rattles the front door
three cats sleep

shoveling snow
barefooted
a crow caws

A Year of Haiku

the winds howl
inside
a dog shakes

scrambling over talus
uphill and down
100 mile trail run

fierce winds
a cat sleeps atop
the heat vent

a moth
circles the lamp
the cats wig out

xylem and phloem
the yoyo
goes up and down

yellow dinosaurs
and red kites
a new quilt

zipper snags
winter break
ends

the cat and dog
swap beds
incessant rain

detached retinas
the cat no longer
leaps

raindrops bouncing
in the hot tub
a sparrow skitters past

flashes
of understanding
tutoring joys

MARCH

waiting
for plum blossoms
the cyclamen blooms

resale shop
the old becomes
another's new

A Year of Haiku

the gazing globe
in the backyard pond
a perplexed dog

mother's hangover
smoking in bed
a childhood ends

finding the
real person under
a student's bravado

waking to
a surprise snow fall
fresh orange juice

a diet of
quilting and reading
daffodils bloom

blaming the full moon
students and teacher
alike

A Year of Haiku

paying bills
the headache never
quits

grey skies
watering hellebores
and daffodils

A Year of Haiku

squaring a quilt
with a rotary cutter
the sun breaks through

a left-handed clock
the student does a
double-take

stars above
soaking in the
hot tub

winter blasts
the approaching spring
a crow caws

first born
arrives two weeks late
Ides of March

family secrets
long held
winter abates

A Year of Haiku

tripping
off the walkway
a four-leaf clover

maple donuts and
video games with my son
Sunday mornings

rectangles into squares
triangles into pinwheels
piecing quilt tops

thundering hail
on the skylight
the vernal equinox

yellow daffodils
purple striped crocuses
a slug meanders

floating
under the stars
hot tub soak

the aerated lawn
full of plugs
a sunny day

a dragonfly
flits above a baby slug
birds chirp

nature's
repeating cycle
a bumblebee returns

rain falling on
pink cyclamen
a crow caws

A Year of Haiku

pouring rain
soaks the dogs
spring break

green tips
on the blue cypress
a robin hunts worms

a dog grinning
a lop-sided smile
the squirrel runs

pencil smears
across the page
a left-hander's mark

sun in my eyes
a cat chases
dust motes

APRIL

the sun teases
before vanishing
April Fool

spring rains
skipped today
a butterfly in the garden

tulip buds
ready to blossom
a frog croaks

a crow overhead
with twigs in her beak
hot tub soak

again
the crow overhead
with twigs in her beak

chickadees
in the birdbath
a rainbow pinwheel spins

the full moon
behind fir trees
a frog croaks

waltzing across
four quilts
my daughter texts

chickadees
building a nest
a cat watches

the splashing
of the fountain
a frog croaks

A Year of Haiku

three frogs
in a mixed chorus
hot tub serenade

peeking through
the tree tops
a hint of mountains

a sunny spot
the cat sleeps
in a new bed

wind chimes sound
the old dog dreams of
summer warmth

quilting anniversary
napping
in my recliner

sharing
my morning shower
eleven slugs

walking under
a low tree branch
water drips inside my collar

a slug resting
on a stair riser
cyclamen bloom

April rains
the birdbath
overflows

April rains
a slug glides
up the fence post

April sun
the cats enjoy
an open window

Earth Day
sitting outside
` reading

a bumblebee
on a pansy
the birds sing

apple blossoms
filling the air
a frog chorus

fig trees
beginning to leaf
slugs on the walkway

apple blossoms
fill the air
a bumblebee flies by

two snails
on the riser
the apple tree blossoms

pink cyclamen
a robin hunts
across the lawn

preening
in the birdbath
black-capped chickadees

clouds swirling
trees bending
hot tub soak

MAY

tree roots
across the lawn
chickadees hop past

pulling the recycling
out to the curb
a crow caws

house fire
the mother
I never knew

the dragon holds
a ruby glass ball
pouring rain

building a nest
beside the backyard pond
black capped chickadees

a Norway Spruce
with bright red cones
two deer run past

a chickadee
in the birdbath
a butterfly flits by

a frog hops
along the pond edge
the crow caws

my home
ruled by a cat
the dogs sleep

a metal ball
floating in the pond
the dog barks

sunrise
soaking in a
hot tub

painting
the deck purple
a hot sunny day

a summer day
the snail moves
along the purple deck

early morning
wake-up call
geese honking

eight lap quilts
in fifteen days
a chickadee in the birdbath

a small snail
sharing my shower
the birds sing

A Year of Haiku

a hummingbird
drinking from the fountain
fish swim past

a cat
batting at himself
mirror reflections

unexpected
Mother's Day gift
magnolia puerh tea

on a ladder
washing skylights
pouring rain

a torrential downpour slugs wander past

stamping papers
hands covered
in purple ink

rains end
dappled sunlight
through fir branches

three quilts
finished and bound
a sunny day

a hummingbird
finds tall blue flowers
holiday weekend

winds whipping
through the firs
a rainbow flag

A Year of Haiku

iridescent wings
catching the sunlight
a dragonfly

picking up
dog poop
a crow caws

napping
in my recliner
a cat snuggles

the cat bats
at the window
an orange butterfly

bees
in the Lithodora
blue skies

JUNE

picking
the first strawberry
a slug moves past

bathing the dog
in the outside shower
pouring rain

floating
in the hot tub
a shooting star

a snail
crawls along
the shower wall

over the roar
of the hot tub jets
birds chattering

fresh strawberries
in the garden
a crow overhead

bringing in
the groceries
the sky drops

a snail
under the hot tub lid
taste for warmth

new tips
on the conifer
a butterfly rests

teaching
the quadratic equation
a monarch butterfly

another round
of novel revisions
chirping birds

nineteen strawberries
from the garden
a crow caws

sitting on
the velociraptor
a robin

my cat
weathering another surgery
sunbreaks

pruning
the Lithodora
a garter snake

body aches
too much gardening
a phone call
from my cat

strong winds
a hummingbird
at the door

three dogs
with matching neckerchiefs
rain turns to sun

mood slips
as bills mount
overwhelming darkness

sharing strawberries
with dogs and slugs
a sunny afternoon

a squirrel races
across the yard
green ginger tea

moving too fast
to photograph
a slug

A Year of Haiku

picking strawberries
between rain showers
the dogs sleep

the dog barks
at a moving branch
only the wind

a sunny lawn
slug trails across
the dog poop

piecing in straight lines
quilting in curves
diversity

in the shower
next to my feet
a slug

a crow
in the birdbath
the dogs bark

a purple house
the dogs
chasing a squirrel

twigs dangle
from the crow's beak
nest building

JULY

a half inch
taller than me
my younger self

sweatshirts
in July
the Pacific Northwest

waking
eye to eye
the cat and me

piecing quilts
for twin girls
two crows bathe

clover
in the grass
a robin hunts worms

the nymph
becomes a laurel
Apollo thwarted

picking strawberries
the dragonfly
takes flight

refilling
the bird bath
another sunny day

a rainbow maker
colored sparkles everywhere
the cat naps

eating breakfast
on the deck
a crow drops by

skimming algae
from the pond
a sparrow drinks

baby robins
around the pond
too many to count

a double arch
holding the birdbath
the robin splashes

a new bedside table
from an old shelf
the cats sleep

A Year of Haiku

watching
a student transform
The Pirates of Penzance

morning fog
fills the ravine
breakfast on the deck

A Year of Haiku

meow, woof
tweet, ack, ack
a new day

a robin hops
along the fence top
dogs bark

early morning thunderstorm staying in bed

Strawberry Festival
watching the parade
with my granddaughter

Strawberry Festival
amusement rides with
my son and granddaughter

a fly
on the rubber duck's head
hot tub soak

text messages
from my son and daughter
a wonderful surprise

cutting diamonds
out of fabric
a robin bathes

faeries hiding
under mushroom caps
baby birds sing

a cat hangs
upside-down
batting a toy

cloudy day
a snail crawls
along the deck

snails and slugs
friends sharing
my outdoor shower

shapes
within shapes
pieced quilt top

rescuing a fly
from the hot tub
a full moon shines

A Year of Haiku

my cat
nearly seventeen
a medical miracle

AUGUST

a tiny body
with the biggest heart
my cat Sasha

a snail
under the shelf
full moon

moonlight
through the bedroom window
a spider web

summer heat
two snails
on the walkway

lethargy settles
over the household
heat wave

floating
in the hot tub
a hummingbird above

A Year of Haiku

a cardinal
in the birdbath
cloudy day

rescuing
a spider from the hot tub
a crow caws

crows cacophony
the cat joins in
a new day

hit and run
injured fawn
mother and twin watch

a snail
on the shower floor
summer breeze

filling
the birdbath
a dragonfly

downward dog
on the deck
birds singing

first one
then another and another
hummingbirds

looking out
the kitchen window
a baby robin

the birth
of an idea
novel revisions

one cracker
two crows
many caws

cleaning soot
from my shower
the neighbor's yard waste fire

in the birdbath
a pair of goldfinches
loads of laundry

surrendering
to the pain
a cat purrs

three chickadees
in the birdbath
a crow caws

removing a sticker
from the new sauna
rainbows on the wall

between the
walkway boards
a slug rises

saying goodbye
to a dear sweet friend
Sasha, the miracle cat

eating candy
on a grassy hill
waving to passing trains

seventeen years
nowhere near
enough time

on the edge
of the hot tub
a frog

publishing
my first novel
fulfilling a dream

A Year of Haiku

tutoring chemistry
a squirrel runs
along the fence

sitting on the fence
students changing
class schedules

a blue jay
on the utility lines
a full moon

SEPTEMBER

a hummingbird
in the fuchsia
new school year

turning on
the heat
summer's end

A Year of Haiku

on the edge of the hot tub a tree frog

a maiden
kissing a frog
finds her princess

snuggling
under two cats
owls hoot

folding laundry
black capped chickadees
in the birdbath

free-motion quilting
a hummingbird
dances in and out

bikers
traveling in packs
a crow caws

bouncing
from task to task
the sun sets

a tree frog
peaking over the edge
hot tub soak

waking
in the night
Jupiter shines

a tree frog
on the hot tub edge
a princess

feeding the cats
a spider moves
along its web

sunset
a robin
in the birdbath

tree
frog
returns
morning
soak

piecing
quilt tops
a crow caws

breathing
more easily
sauna heat

yard sculptures
a penguin and a giraffe
the work week ends

tutoring
an   orange sky
as the sun sets

spider webs
dangle over
my shower

sparrows dodge
in and around the fountain
a frog croaks

a tree frog
behind the soap dish
cyclamen bloom

a robin
sits atop a hemlock
the sunset's red rays

hot tub
and shower
homes for frogs

the robin sitting
on a concrete frog
a hummingbird

bees hopping
flower to flower
the temperature drops

reaching for the handle a snail

opening
the hot tub lid
a full moon

opening
the front door
a hummingbird

talking
to my deaf cat
the dog barks

OCTOBER

the woodpecker
on the utility pole
a squirrel jumps

a hole
in the closet door
cat portal

glass-topped desk
the cats steps
uncertainly

the weight of the world
too soon
a freshman's suicide

two frogs
in the hot tub and shower
an island mourns

a plump robin
in the birdbath
the cat watches

A Year of Haiku

sitting
in the sauna
joined by a cat

gently lifting
the hot tub lid
a tree frog sleeps

front yard
awash in birds
the cat sleeps

piecing
a quilt top
the cat helps

tutoring a student
a robin splashes
in the birdbath

one quarter
of a quilt top
the cat watches

dew drops
on spider webs
hot tub soak

pine needles
floating in the hot tub
autumn winds

a sandwich
for dinner
power outage

racing
to an appointment
a slug on the walkway

wet feet
tracking pine needles
autumn storm

school budget
no money for books
a crow caws

a small slug
above the soap dish
morning shower

falling raindrops
making bubbles
hot tub soak

clouds drift
soaring overhead
a crow caws

the slug glides
below the shower handle
a flock of birds

A Year of Haiku

a cat's whiskers
tickle my cheek
morning alarm

first tattoos
mother son
bonding

gliding
along the shower wall
a banana slug

a tree frog
scooting under the hot tub
winter approaches

warping my loom
green on green
the cat watches

pine needles
on shower shelves
sunbreak

A Year of Haiku

plotting
my next novel
a frog croaks

waiting
at the sauna door
my cat

one day
two inches of rain
dogs howl

NOVEMBER

cloud cover
the full moon
darting in and out

again
and again
the sky drops

A Year of Haiku

streams
in the backyard
a frog croaks

crows
in the firs
caw after caw

the rubber duck
sailing across the hot tub
windy night

out of the fog
steam rising
from the hot tub

A Year of Haiku

tutoring
a student
the light dawns

rescuing
a spider
from the cat

waning moon
frost settles
on the roof

frost
on the hot tub lid
morning soak

joined by
a tree frog
morning soak

getting the mail
in the dark
slugs on the walkway

a cloudy morning
flakes of paint
in the hot tub

two cats
sleeping curled together
pouring rain

fir needles
on the skylights
a dog barks

high above
a cat pounces
the room shakes

sunbreaks
between cloud bursts
two inches of rain

fresh lakes
in the backyard
record rains

sunlight
strikes the rainbow flag
storm debris

looking
at Saturn
looking at me

snuggling
with my fur friends
temperatures drop

a cup of tea
half inch by half inch
winter rains

the cat
stealing raw spinach
nearly a full moon

rearranging
the cat furniture
wind in the firs

hot tub steam
a lawnmower breaks
the silence

between Jupiter
and the full moon
a fir tree

A Year of Haiku

a summer day
her little hand in mine
granddaughter's visit

washing dishes
the full moon centered
in the window

turning the corner
the wind and rain
in my face

firs drip
rain into my collar
a walk to the mailbox

DECEMBER

fir branches
twisting in the wind
a dog barks

washing dog poop
off the deck
a fuchsia

a quiet afternoon
three dogs
at the groomers

wind in the firs
a flock of bird
takes flight

firs swaying
across the sky
white tracks

a fallen branch
on the lawn
holiday lights

one cat
stalks the other
furniture jungle

putting up
indoor lights
a cat helps

A Year of Haiku

the spider
climbs the purple post
a coyote howls

high in the firs
a single bird calls
morning soak

a mountain top
through the clouds
the dog sleeps

holiday lights
on the penguin and giraffe
a pink cyclamen

night walk
to the mailbox
stepping over the slugs

voices
forever silenced
the world weeps

chickadees
chasing being chased
wind in the firs

a maple leaf
on the deck
falling rain

floating
in the hot tub
the firs sway

bird songs
echoing in the firs
a light dusting of snow

framed drawing
a holiday gift
from friends

chickadees
darting fir to fir
morning shower

sitting
on the neighbor's roof
mountain peaks

wrapping presents lights twinkle in anticipation

resetting
the holiday lights
a slug

playing faeries
with my granddaughter
the cats sleep

heavy rains
with a few snowflakes
Christmas morning

adding water
to the hot tub
the birds sing

piecing
a quilt top
chirping birds

folding laundry
my new bracelet
jingles

a halo
surrounds the full moon
cloudy night

a robin
in the birdbath
sunbreak

picking up
months of poop
a crow caws

ABOUT THE AUTHOR

Daphne Ashling Purpus lives on Vashon, a small rural island community just west of Seattle, with her three dogs and three cats. She is a volunteer tutor and librarian at Student Link, Vashon's alternative high school, and also an avid quilter, making what she calls "Portable Hugs," lap quilts for anyone who could use a hug. She has recently published her first novel, Dragon Riders. A Year of Haiku is her first published collection of haiku. She plans to have her second novel published later this year.

www.ingramcontent.com/pod-product-compliance
Lightning Source LLC
Chambersburg PA
CBHW071403090426
42737CB00011B/1326